Hi! My name is Eddie.
My name is
AF584733

Track your progress. Help Eddie collect all the prizes.
Find and track the letter to match your completed page.
Colour the prizes.

i
j
f
z
x
WOW!
d
g
a
e
q
s
p
k
GREAT WORK

Posture

Lower back supported by the chair

Feet flat on the floor

Paper position

Left-handed

Non-writing hand steadies the paper

Right-handed

Pencil grip

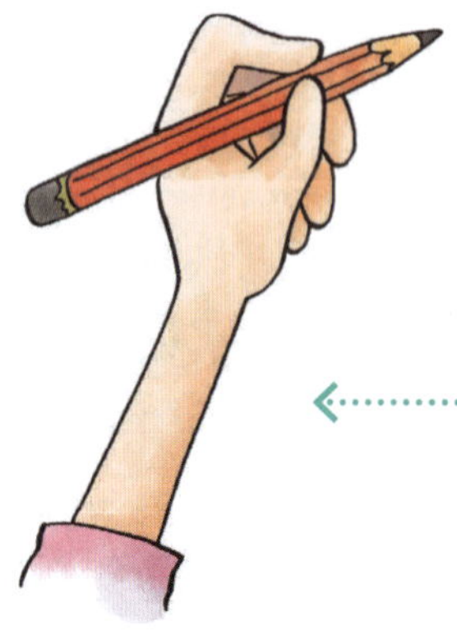

Left-handed

Hold your pencil like this. (Not too tightly!)

Right-handed

I am Eddie.

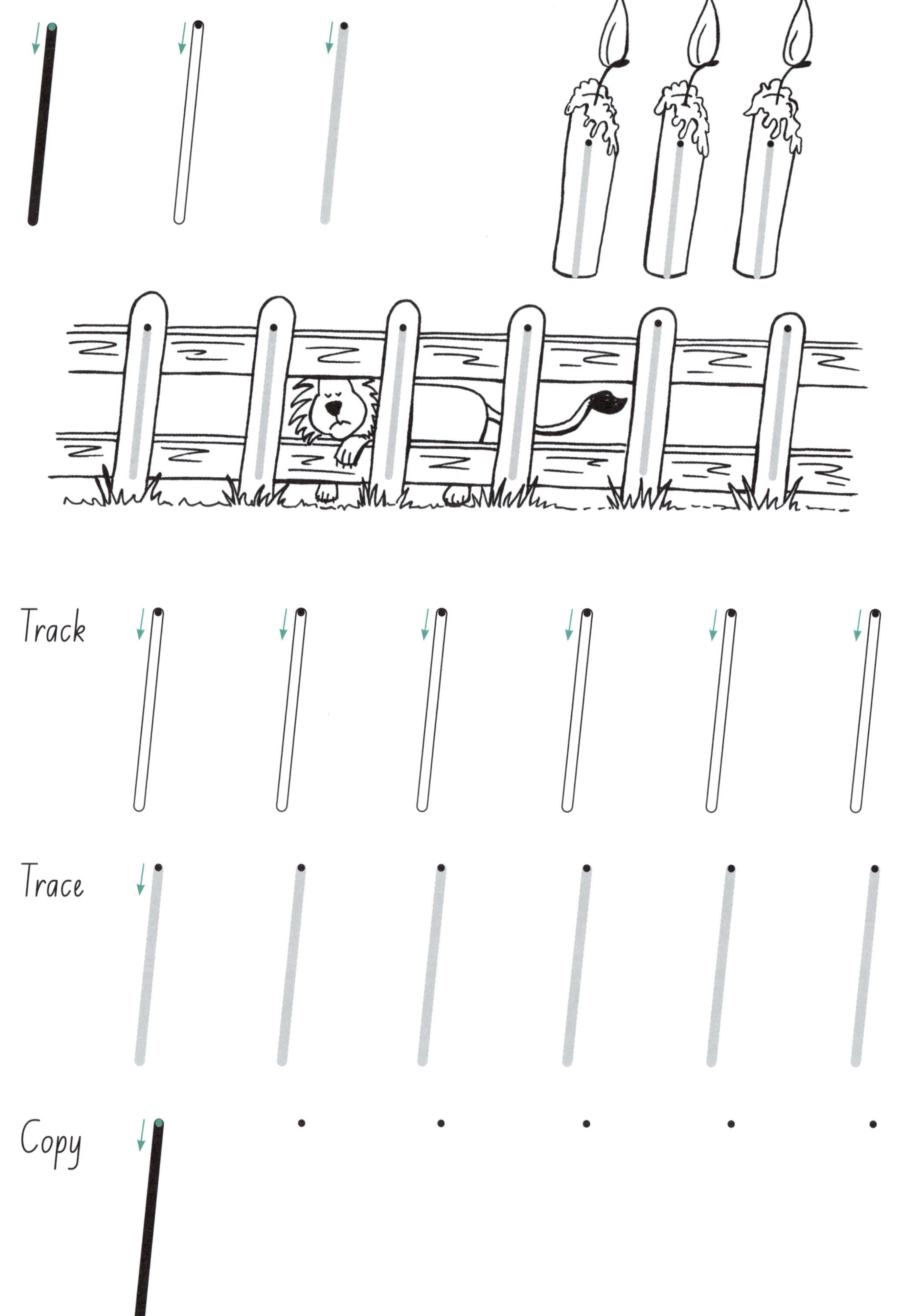
Track
Trace
Copy

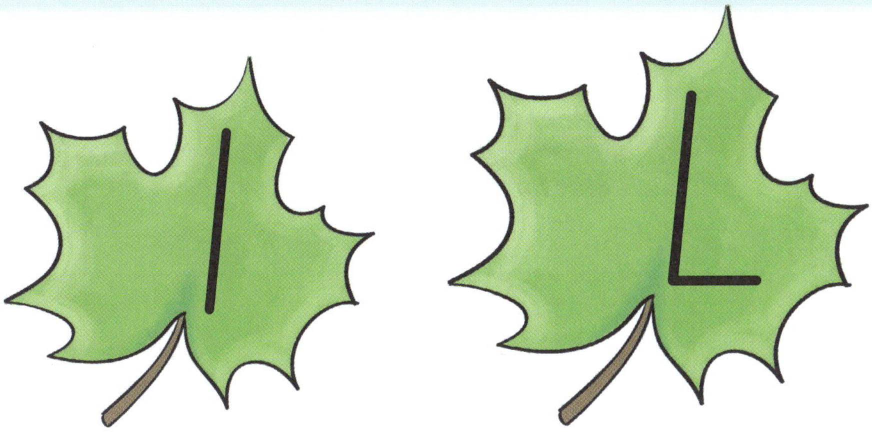

l L

l l l l l l

above

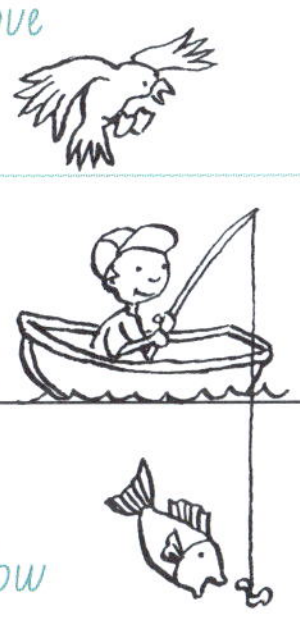

on

below

l l l l l

like

Do you **like** my tree house?

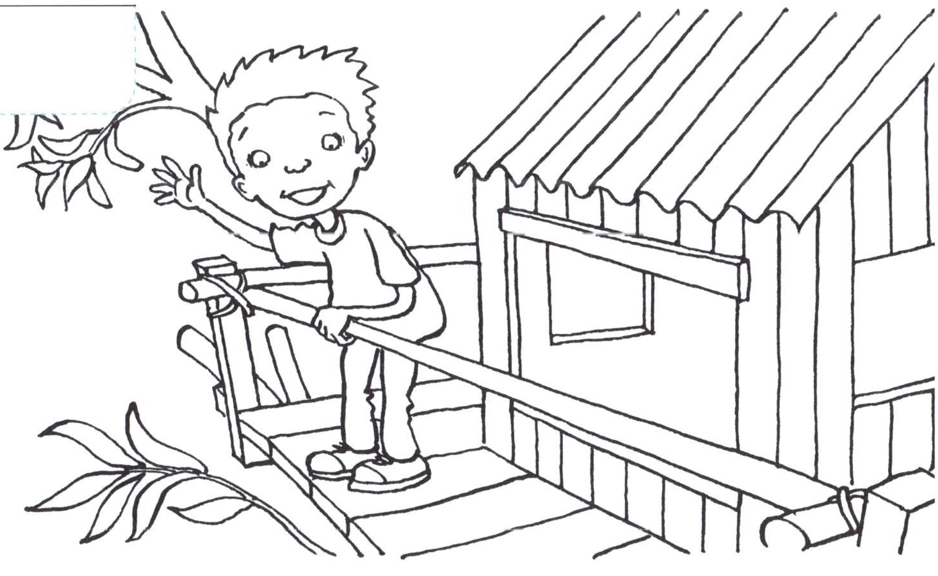

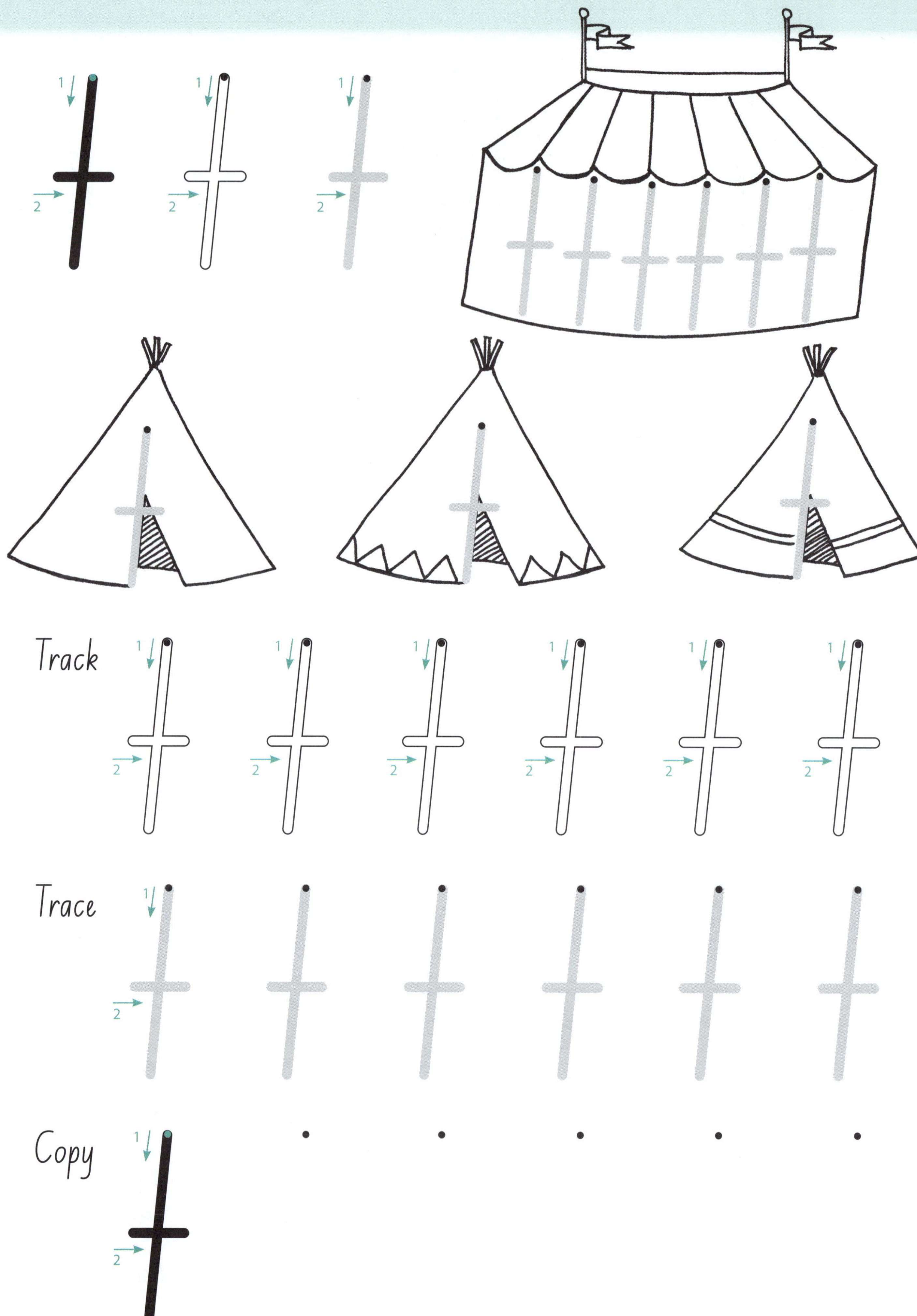

Track

Trace

Copy

t T

above

on

below

there

There is my mum and my dad.

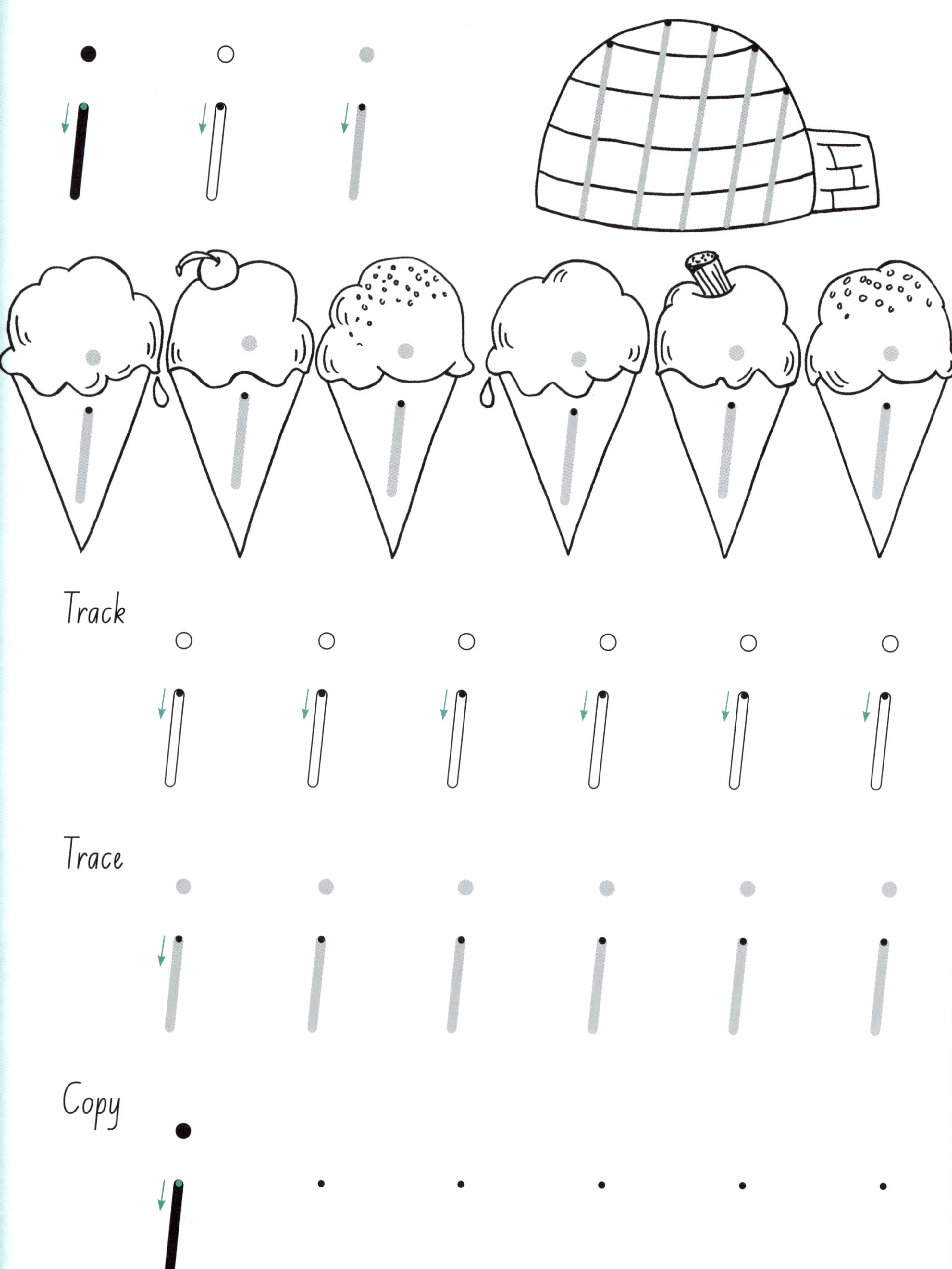
Track
Trace
Copy

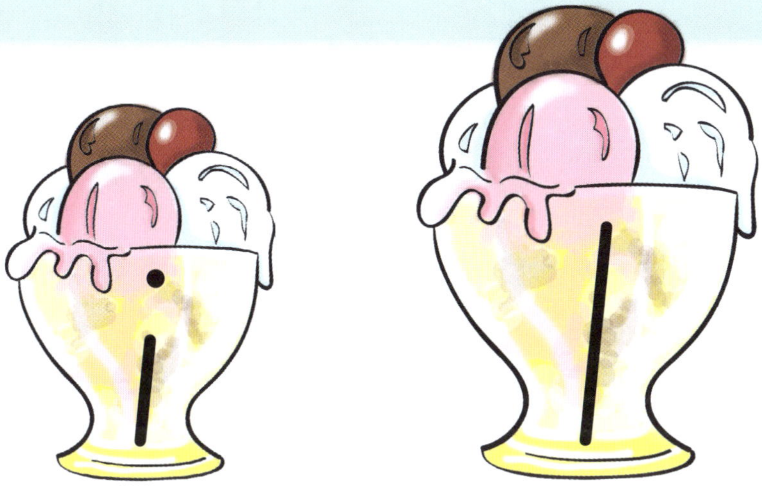

i l

i i i i i i

above
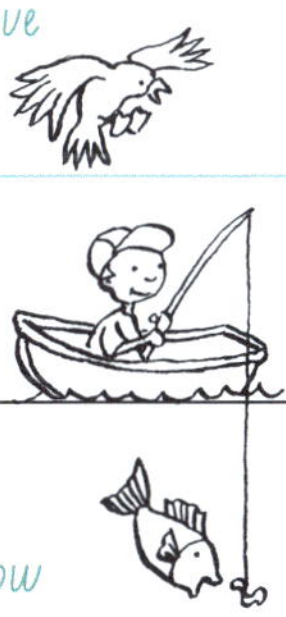
on
below

i i i i i

is

There **is** Star, my dog.

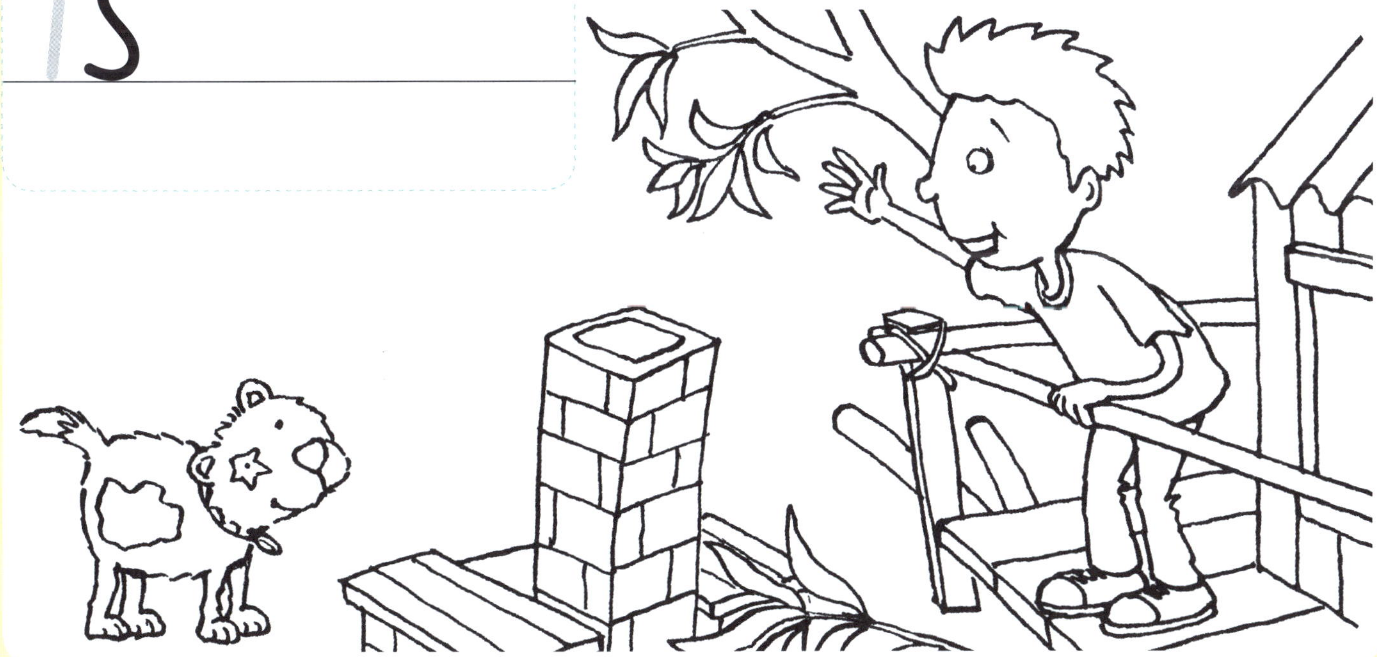

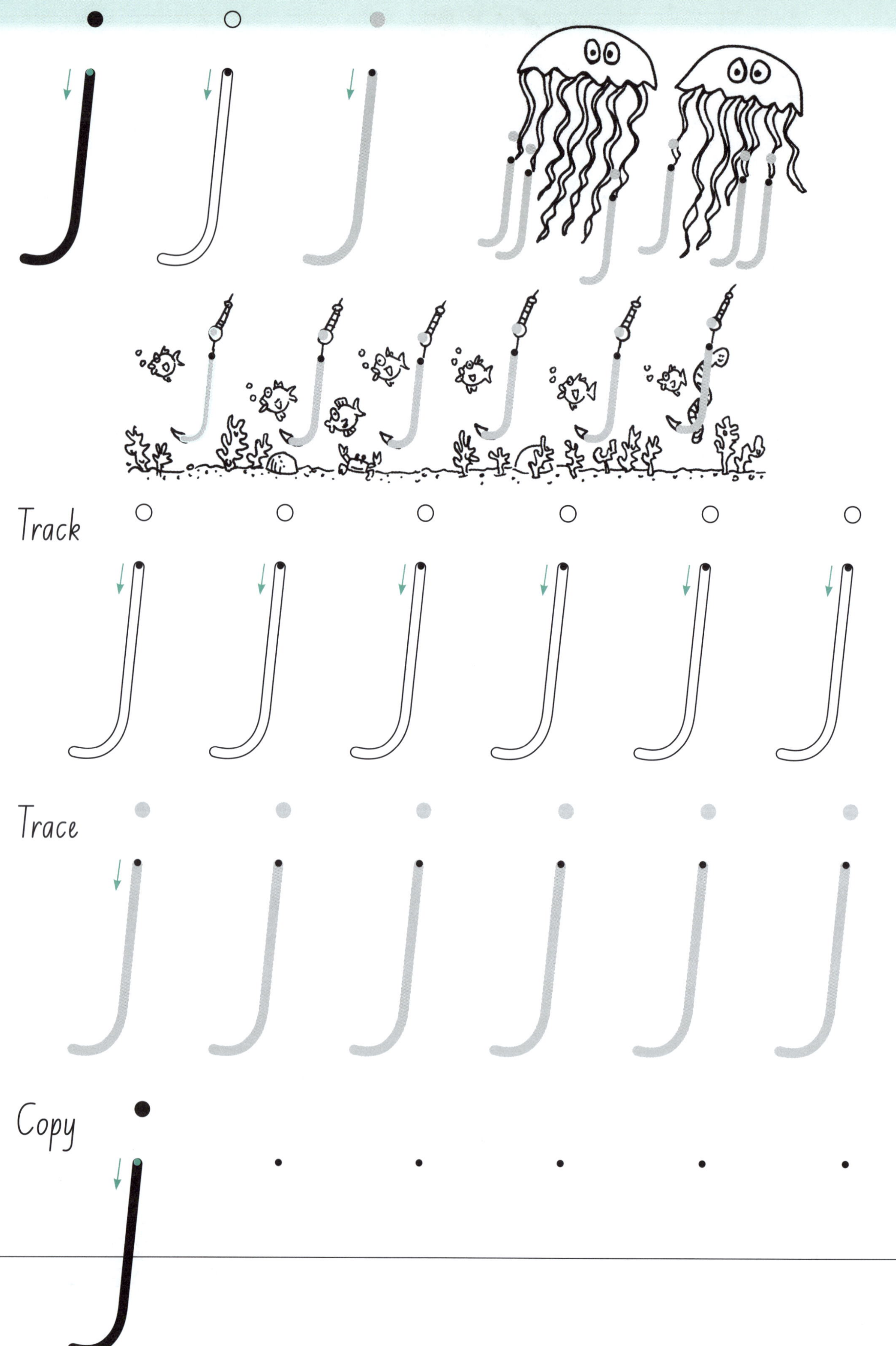
Track
Trace
Copy

j J

j J

j j j j j j

above

on

below

j j j j j

just

I **just** saw my sister, Pippa.

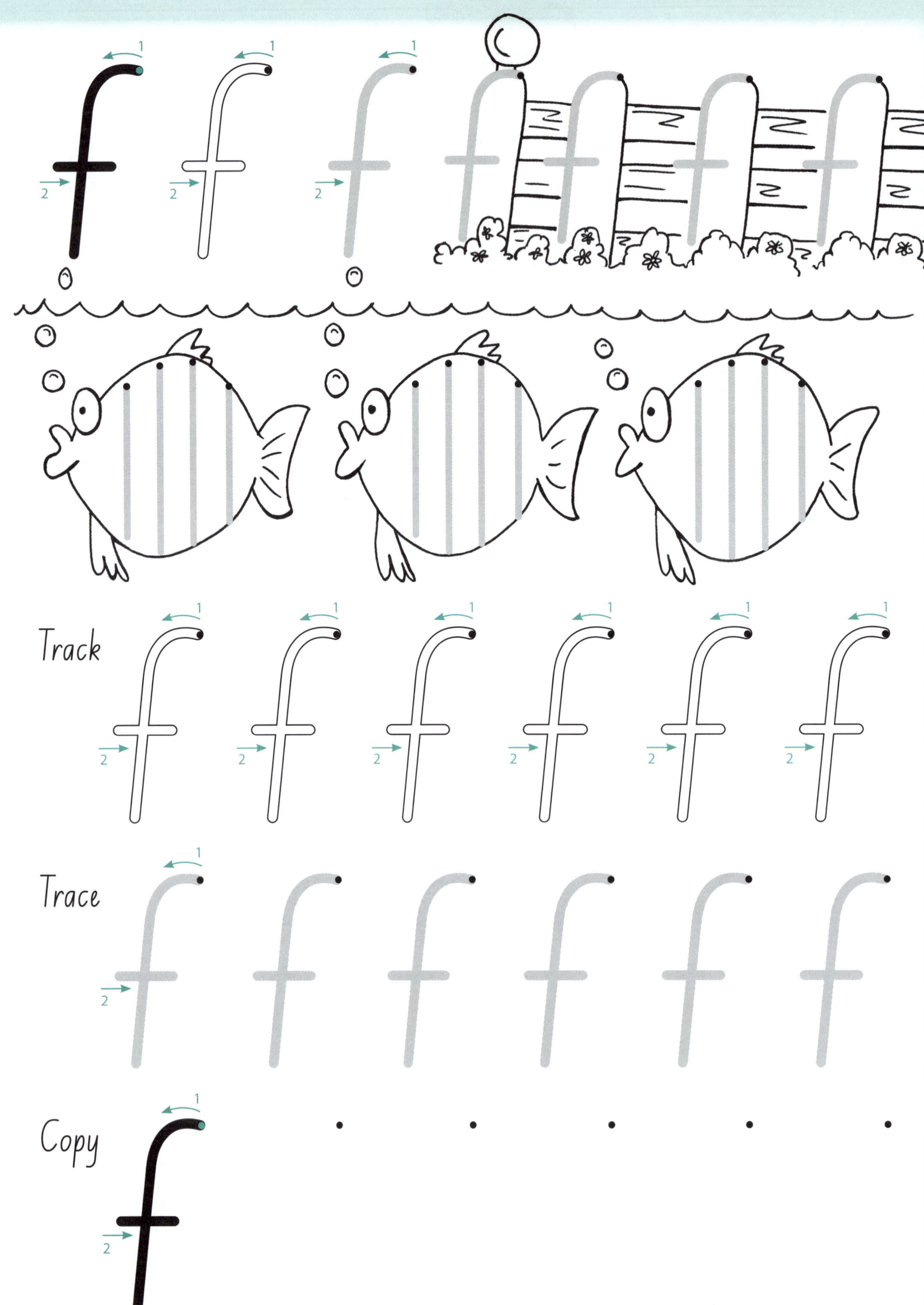
1
2
Track
Trace
Copy

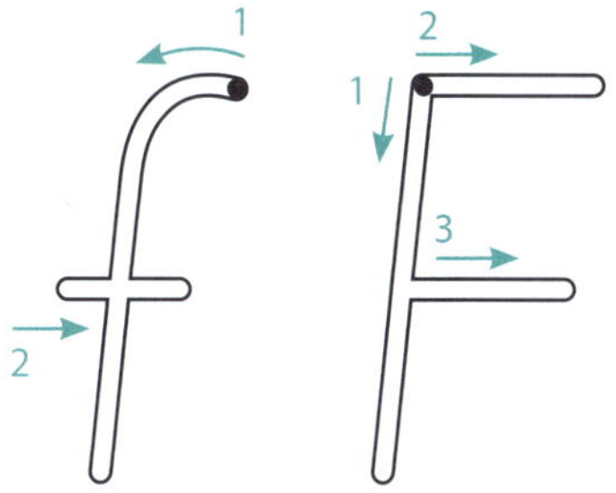

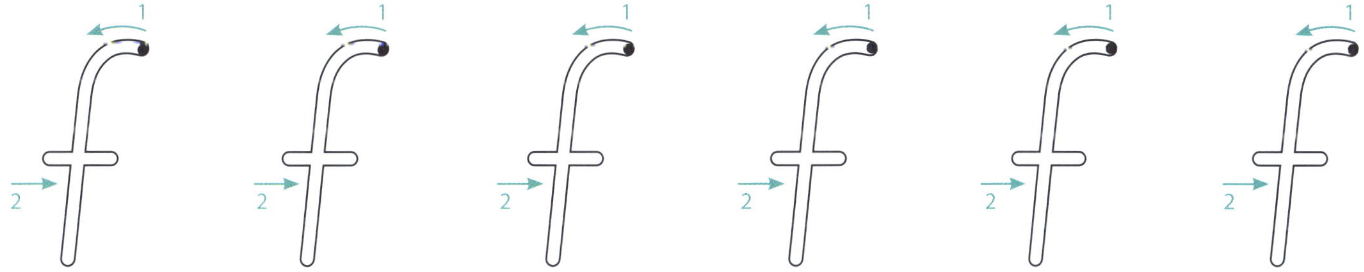

f F

1 2 f

2 1 F 3

1 f 2 (×6)

above

on

below

f f f f f

for

No dinner **for** me tonight!

Track

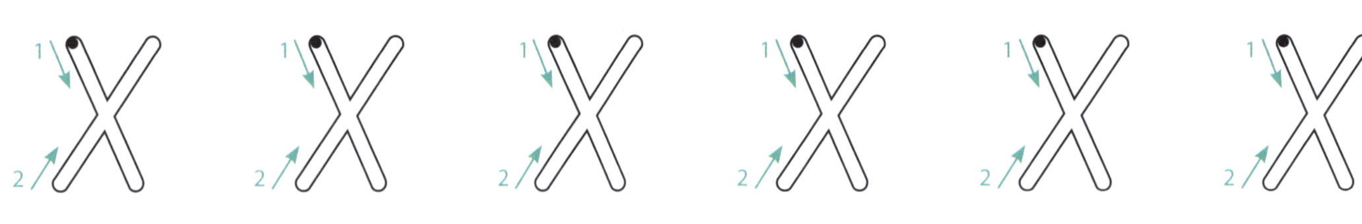

Trace

Copy

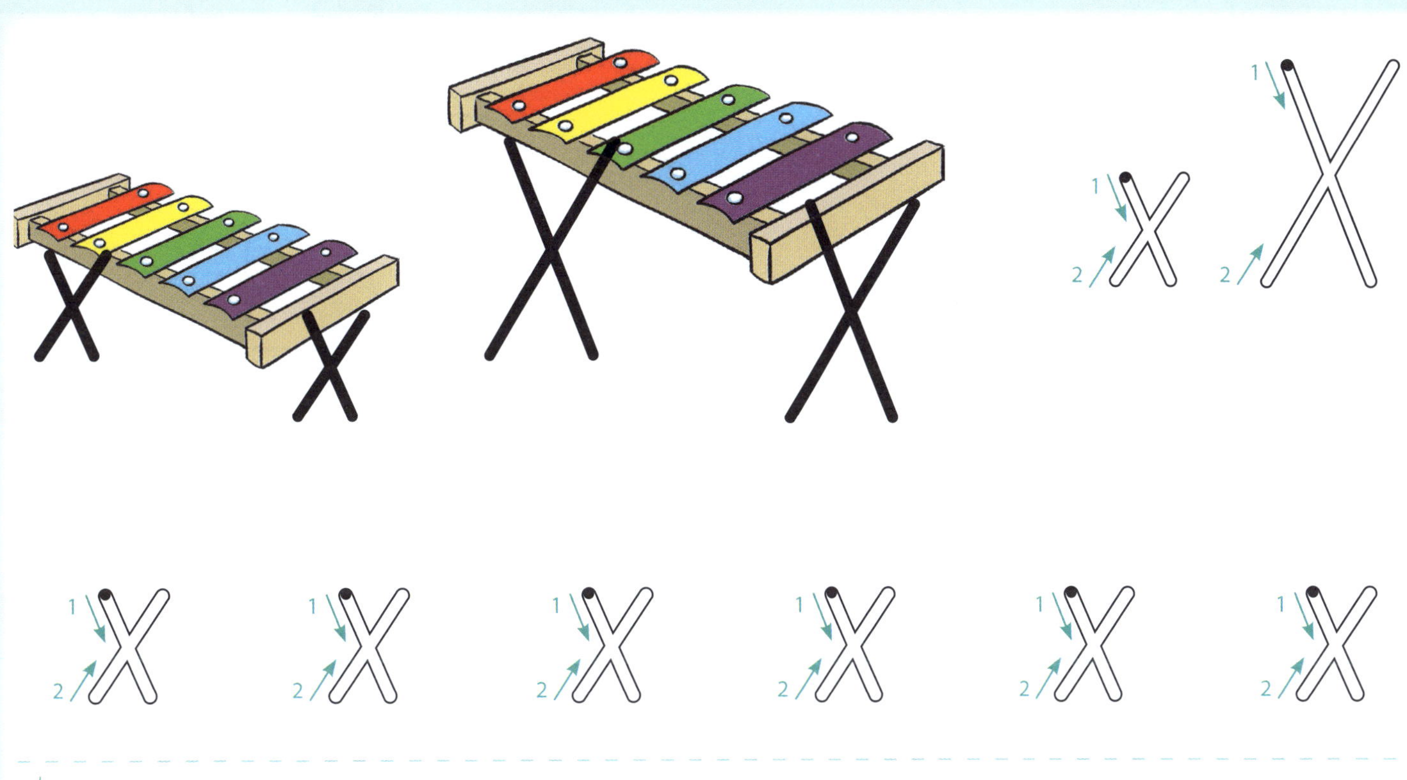

above

on

below

It was my birthday. I was **six**.

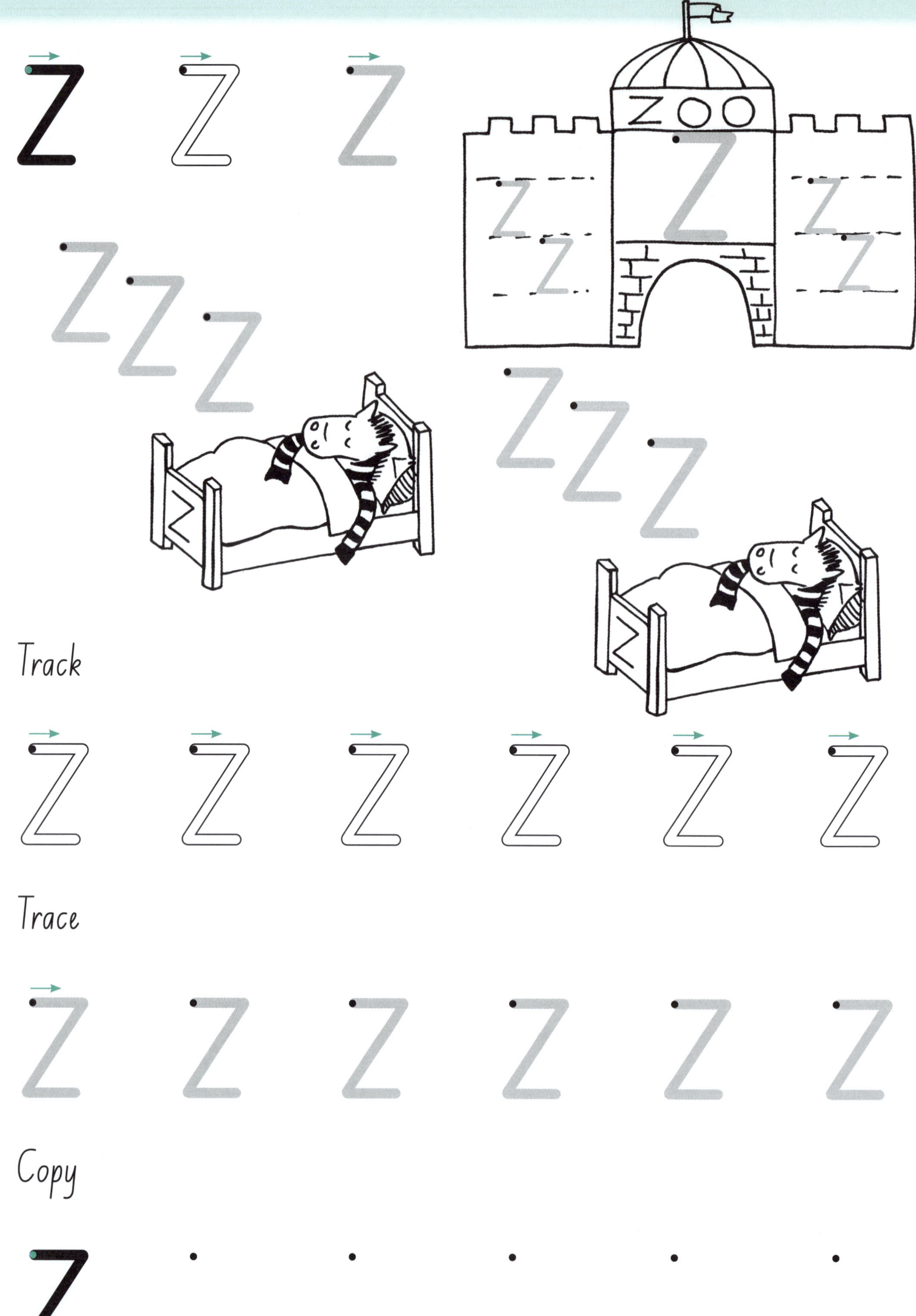

Track

Trace

Copy

z Z

z Z

z z z z z z

above

on

below

z z z z z

zoo

I went to the **zoo** with my family.

Track

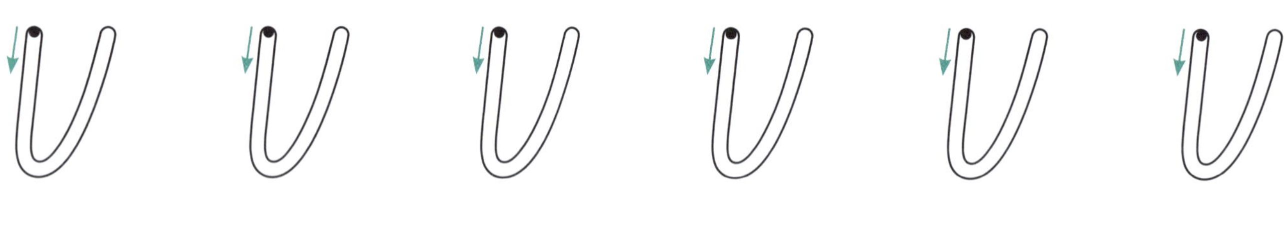

Trace

Copy

u v

u u u u u u

above

on

below

u u u u u

very

The monkeys were **very**, **very** funny.

w w w

www www www

www www

Track

w w w w w w

Trace

w w w w w w

Copy

w

W w

w w w w w w

above

on w w w w w

below

went

We **went** to see the wild animals.

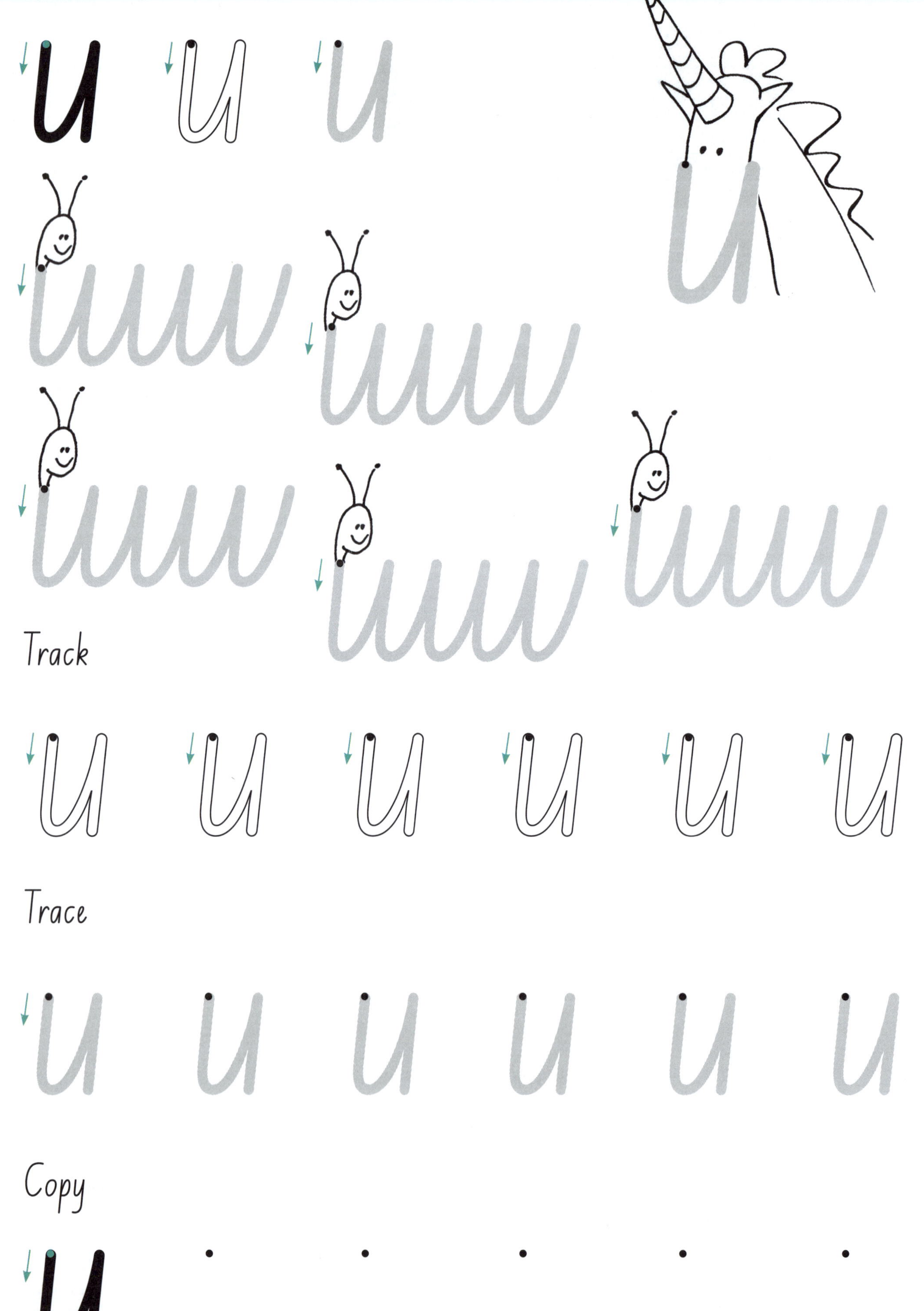

Track

Trace

Copy

u U u U

u u u u u u

above

on u u u u u

below

until

We stayed at the zoo **until** lunchtime.

Track

Trace

Copy

y Y

1 2

y Y

y y y y y y

above

on

below

y y y y y

your

"Look, there is **your** new friend," said Mum.

Track

Trace

Copy

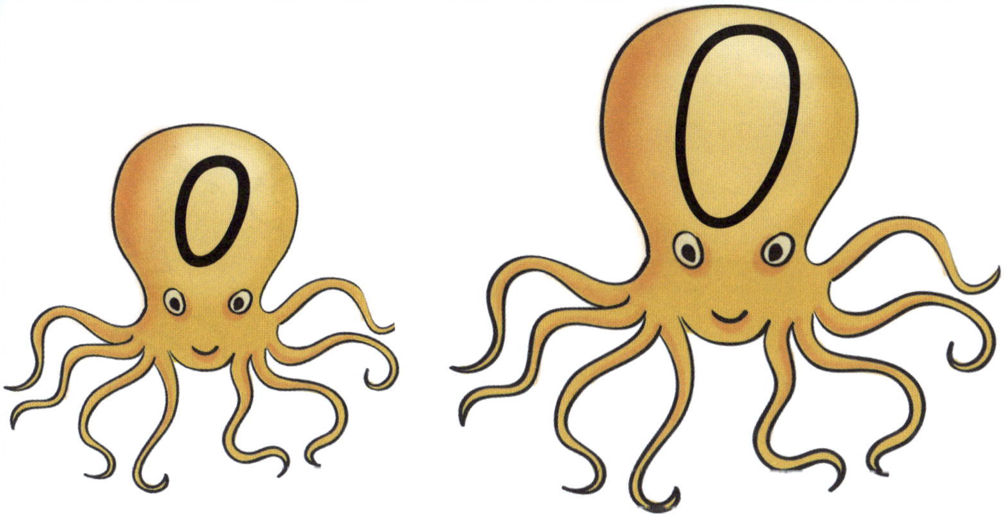

o O

o o o o o o

above

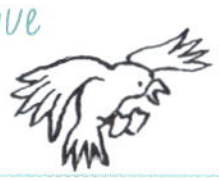

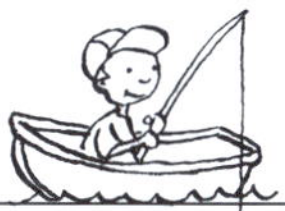

on o o o o o

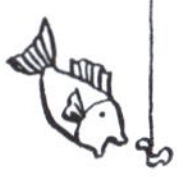

below

over

"Come **over** to my house," I said.

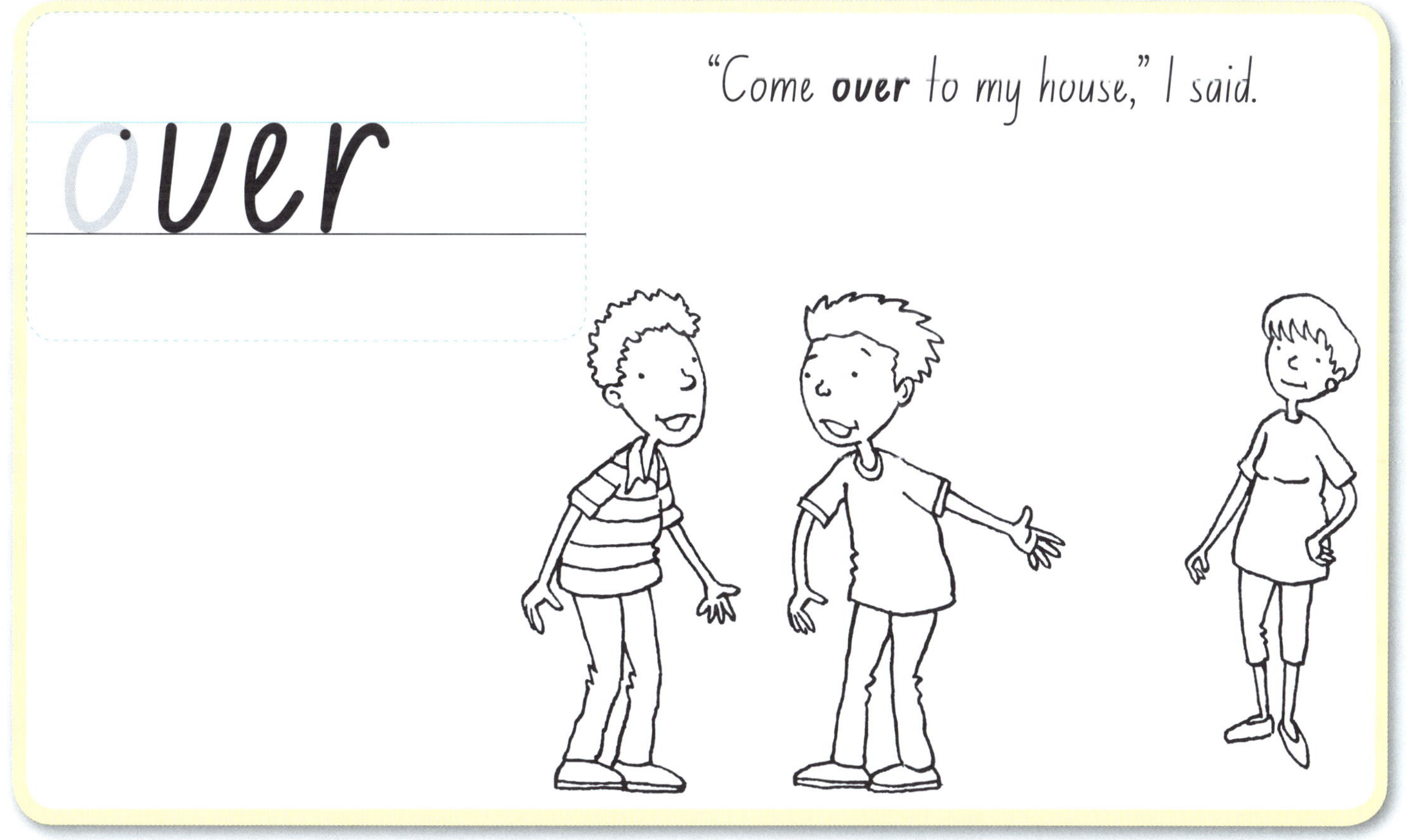

c c c

Track

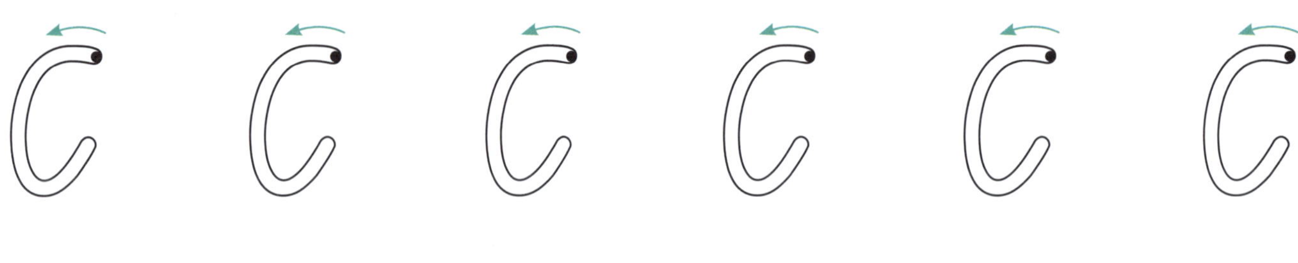

Trace

Copy

c C

c c c c c c

above

on c c c c c

below

came

My new friend **came** to play.

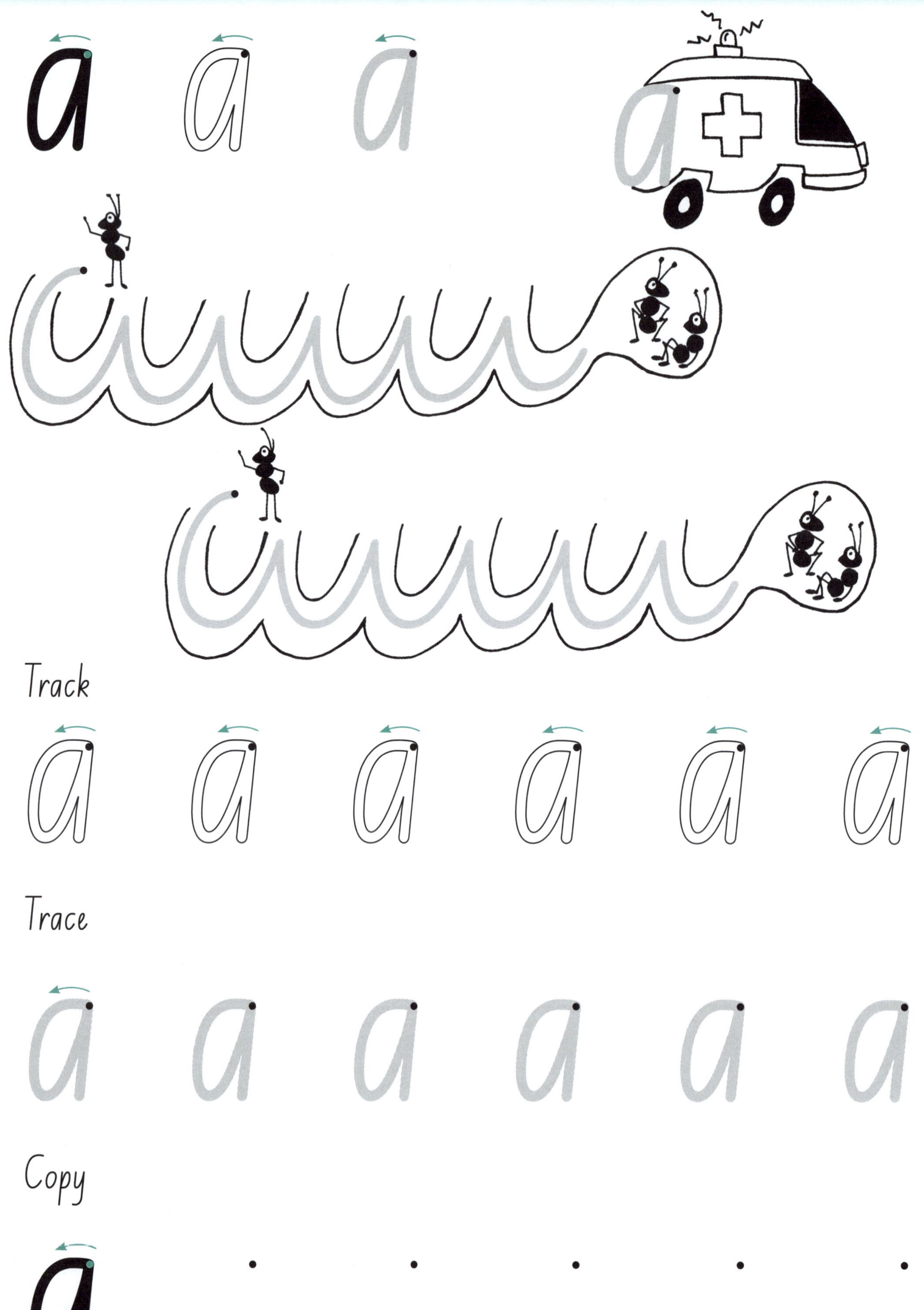

Track

Trace

Copy

a A

a A

1 2 3

a a a a a a

above

on

below

a a a a a

and

We had sandwiches **and** grapes.

d d d

d

Track

d d d d d d

Trace

d d d d d d

Copy

d

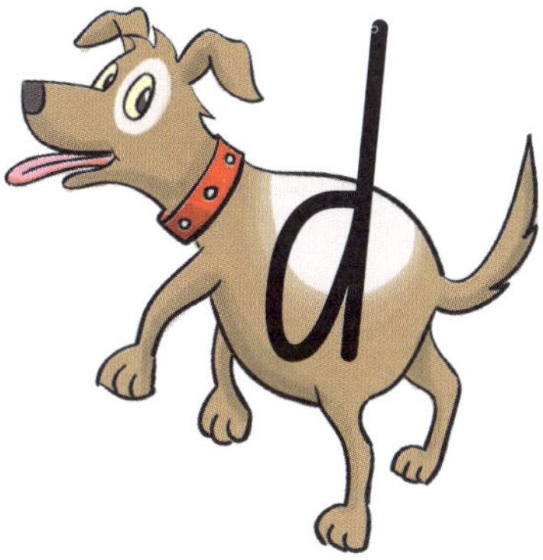

d 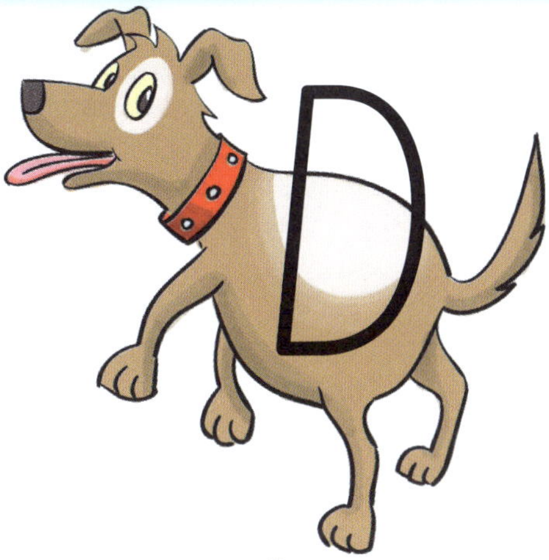 D d D

d d d d d d

above

on

below

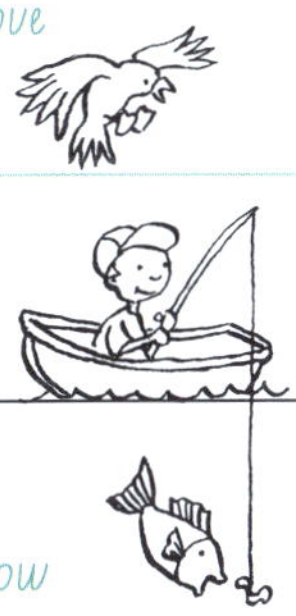

d d d d d

g g g g

g g g g g

Track g g g g g g

Trace g g g g g g

Copy g

g G
above
on
below
go
"Can we **go** into my bedroom to play?"

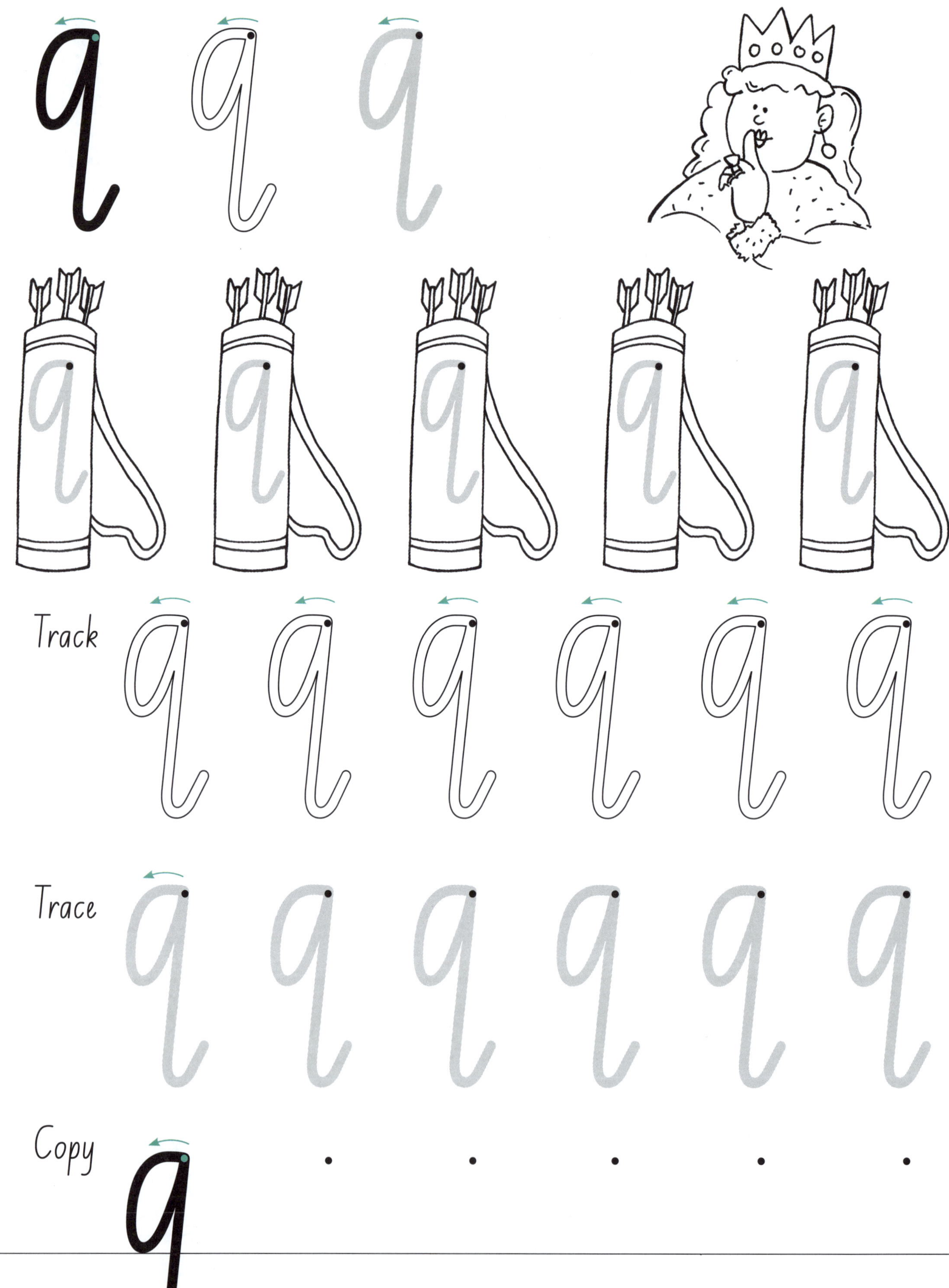
Track
Trace
Copy

q
Q
1
2
q q q q q q q
above
on
below
q q q q q
quiet
"You can play a **quiet** game in your room," said Mum.

Track

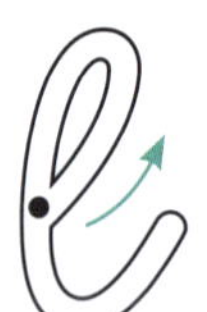 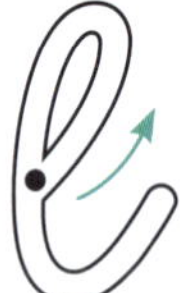 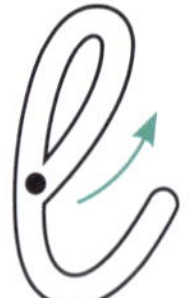   

Trace

Copy

e E e E

e e e e e e

above

on e e e e e

below

ever

"Did you **ever** see such a mess?" said Mum.

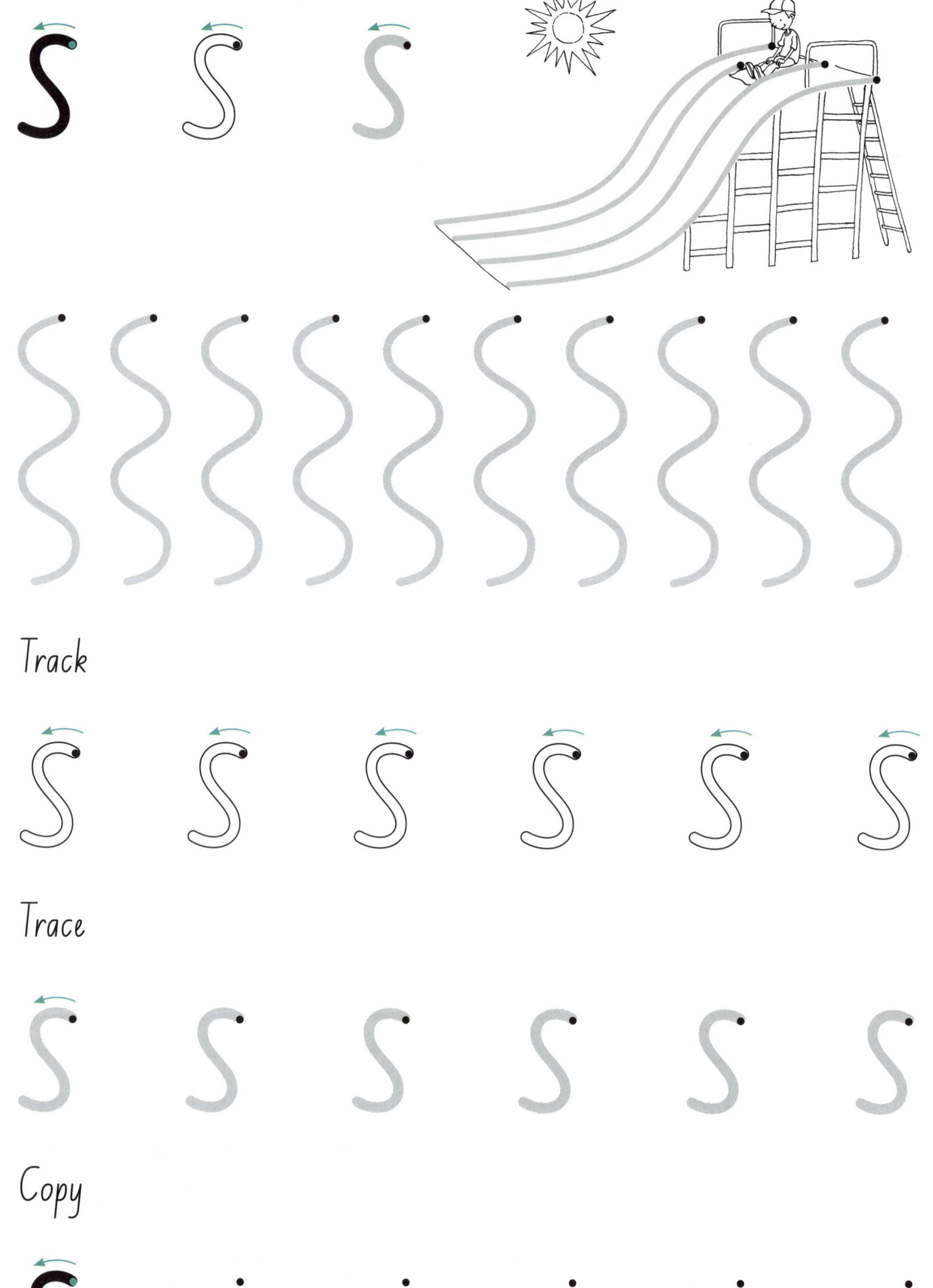

Track

Trace

Copy

My mum was **so** cross!

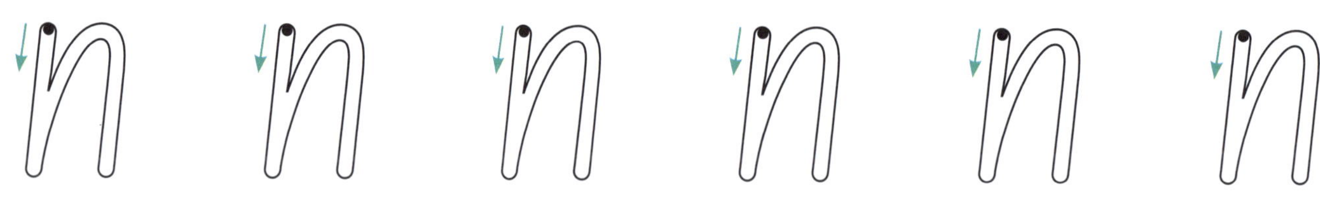

Track

n n n n n n

Trace

n n n n n n

Copy

n

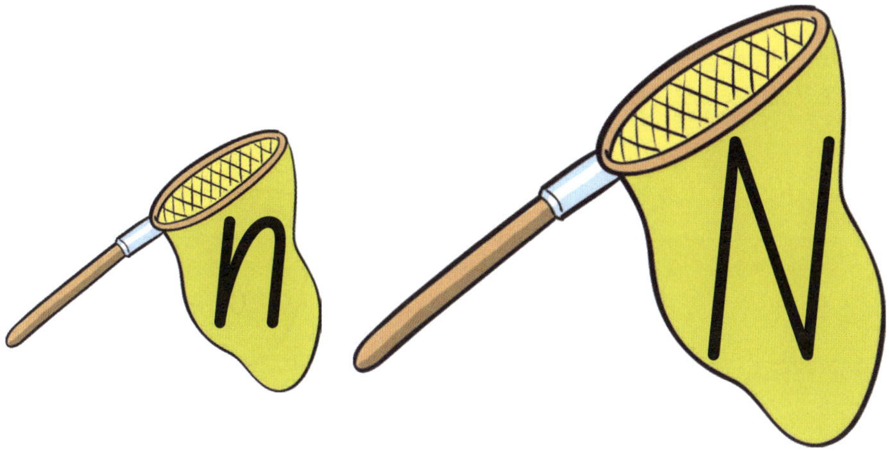

n N

n N

n n n n n n

above

on

below

n n n n n

night

I cleaned my room the very next **night**.

Track

m m m m m m

Trace

m m m m m m

Copy

m

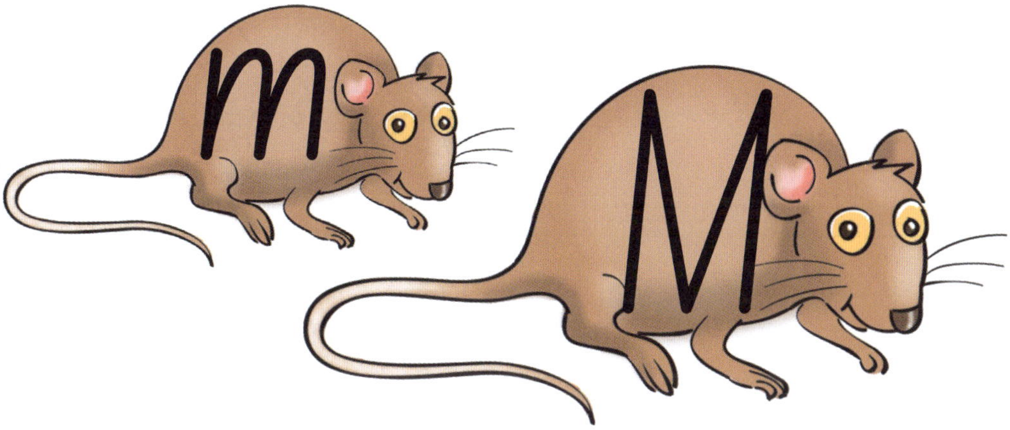

m M m M

m m m m m m

above

on m m m m m

below

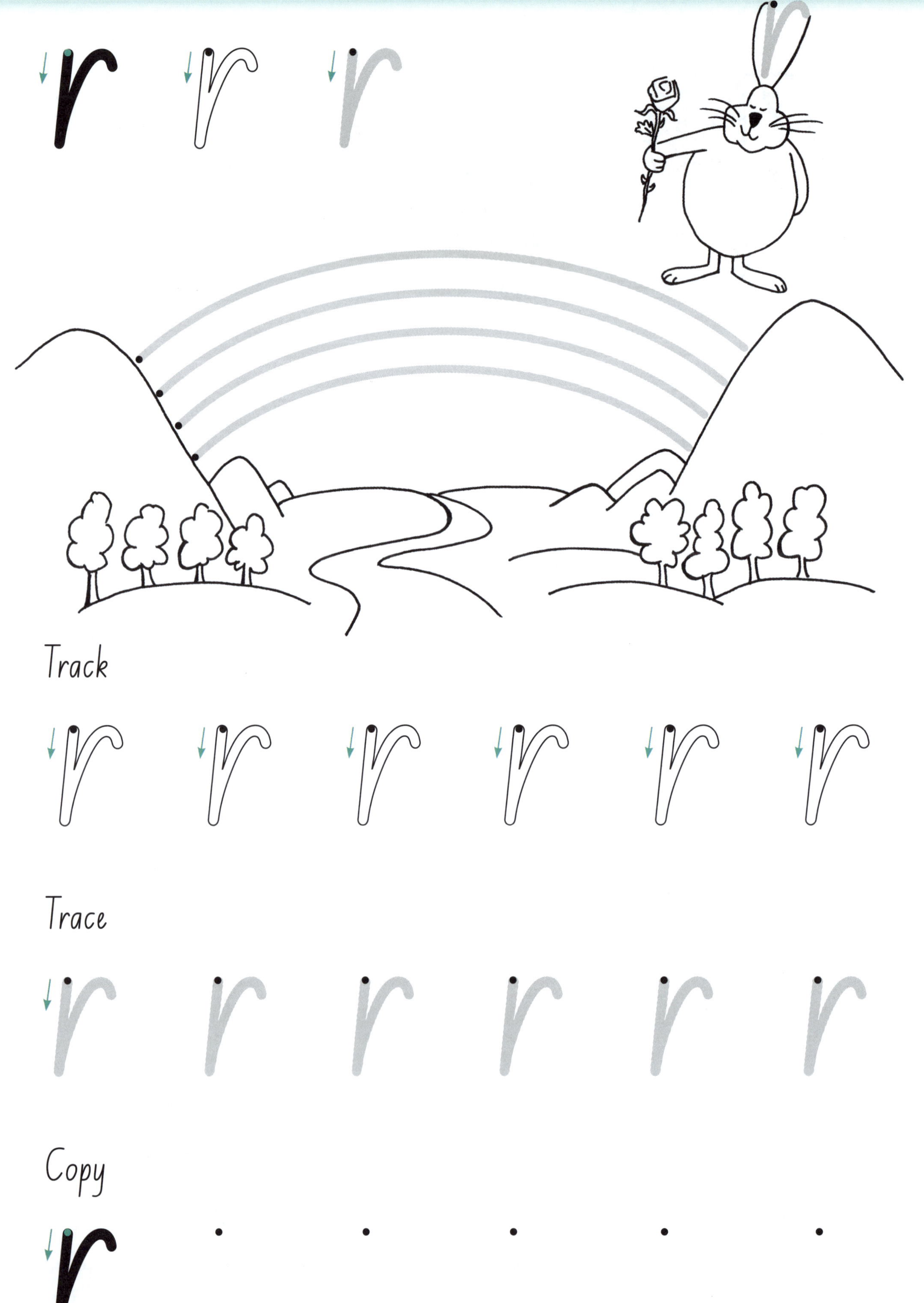
r r r
Track
r r r r r r
Trace
r r r r r r
Copy
r

r R

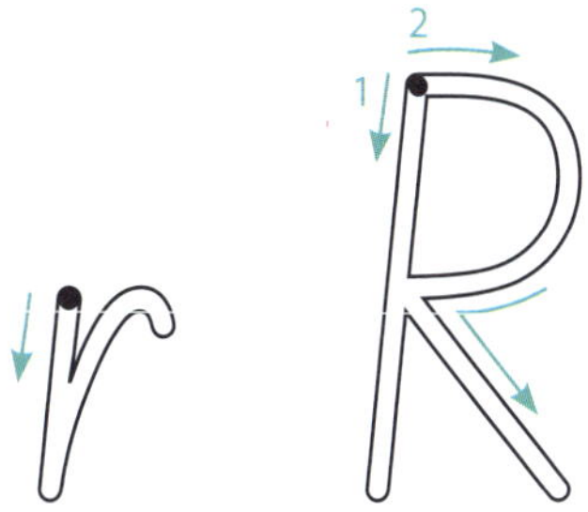

r R

r r r r r r

above

on

below

r r r r r

really

"You are a **really** good boy, Eddie," she said.

h h h

Track h h h h h h

Trace h h h h h h

Copy h

h H

h H

h h h h h h

above

on

below

h h h h h

had

I **had** to get up early because I was going to school.

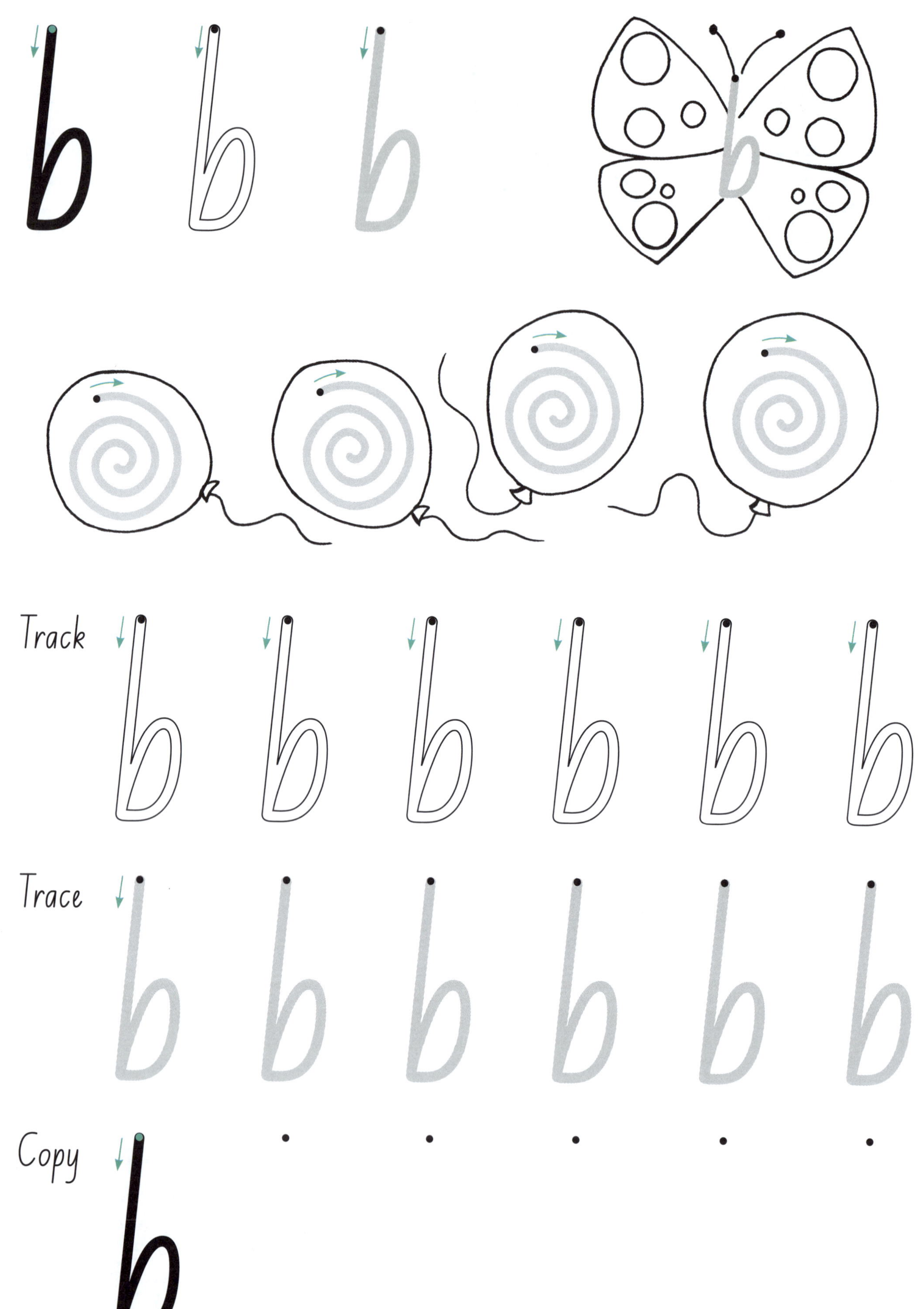
Track
Trace
Copy

be

"I can't **be** late today because I'm getting an award."

Track

Trace

Copy

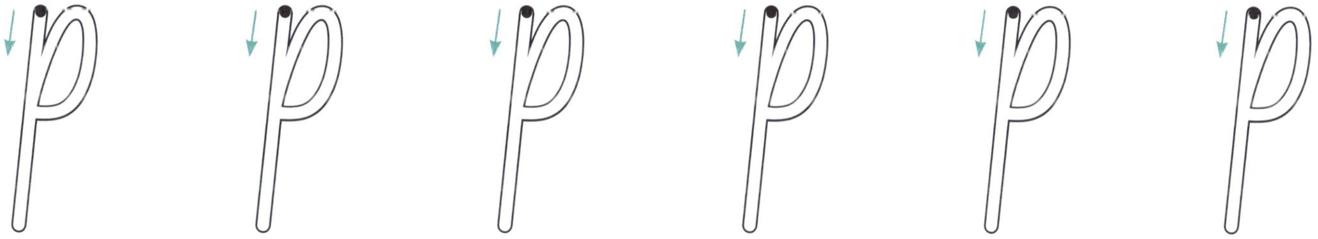

p P p P

p p p p p p

above

on

below

p p p p p

played

I was early, so I **played** soccer before school.

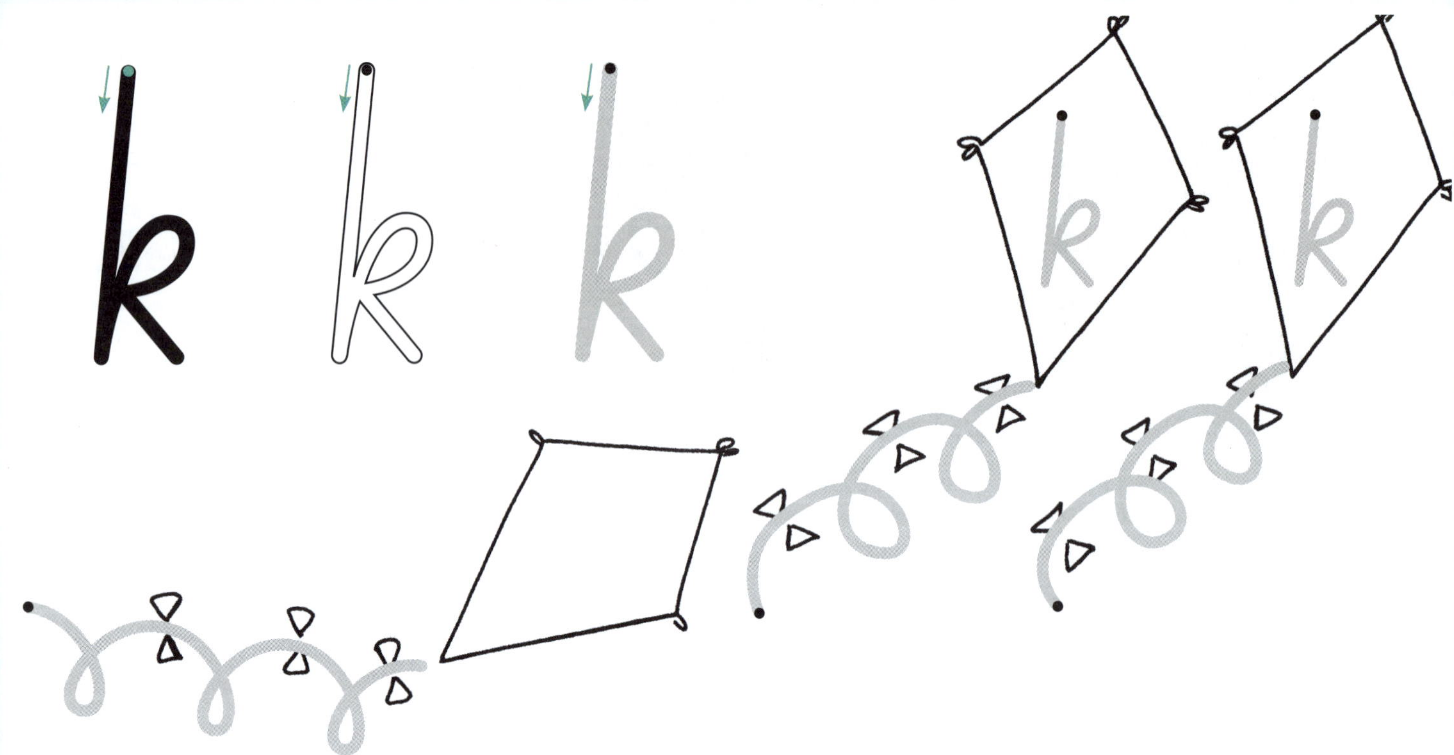

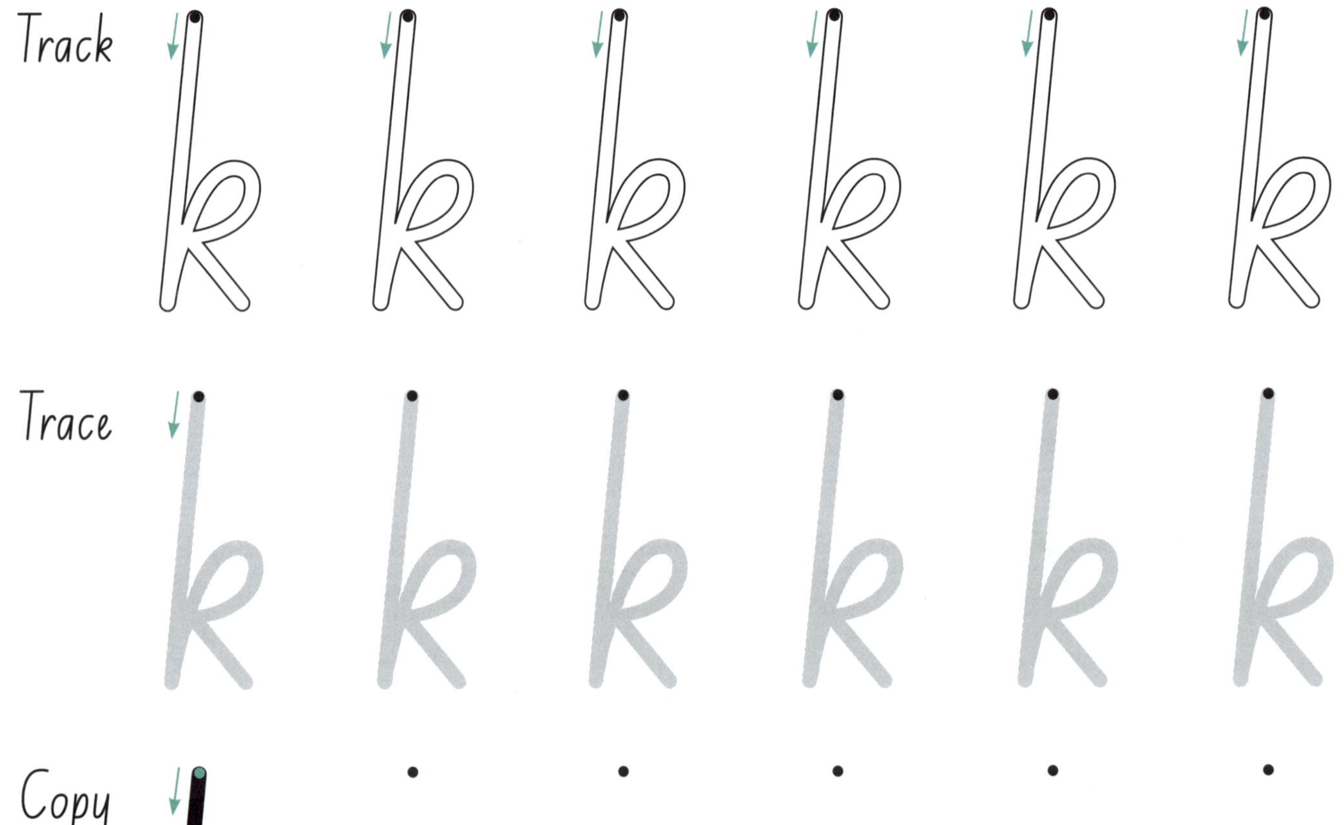
Track
Trace
Copy

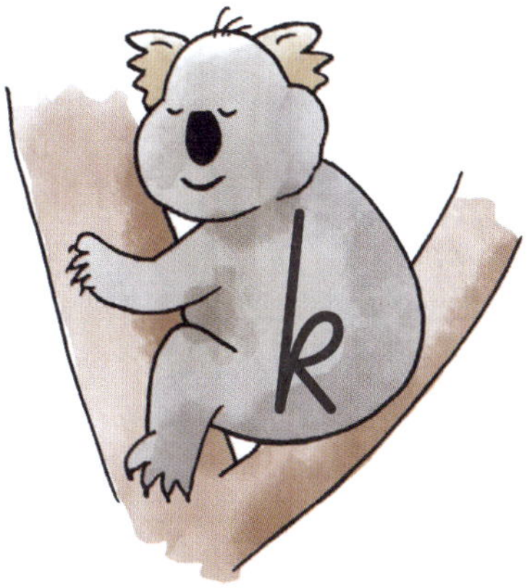

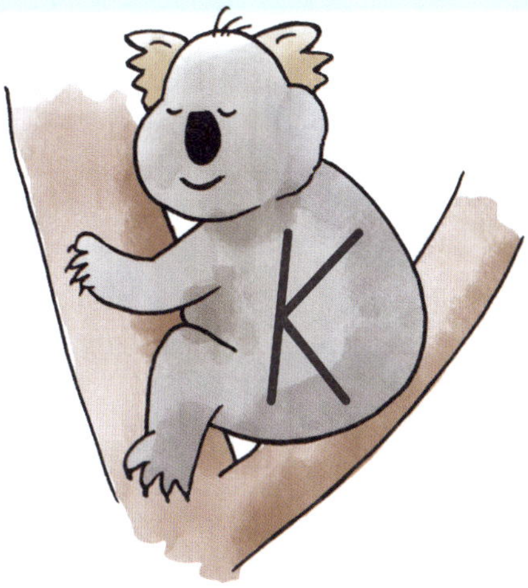

k K

k k k k k k

above

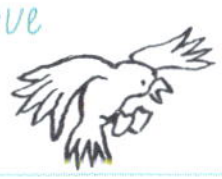

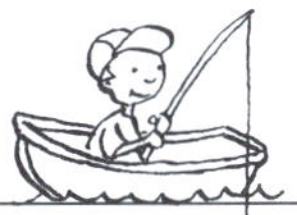

on

k k k k k

below

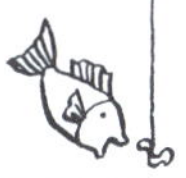

know

Do you **know** what time it is?

It's award time!

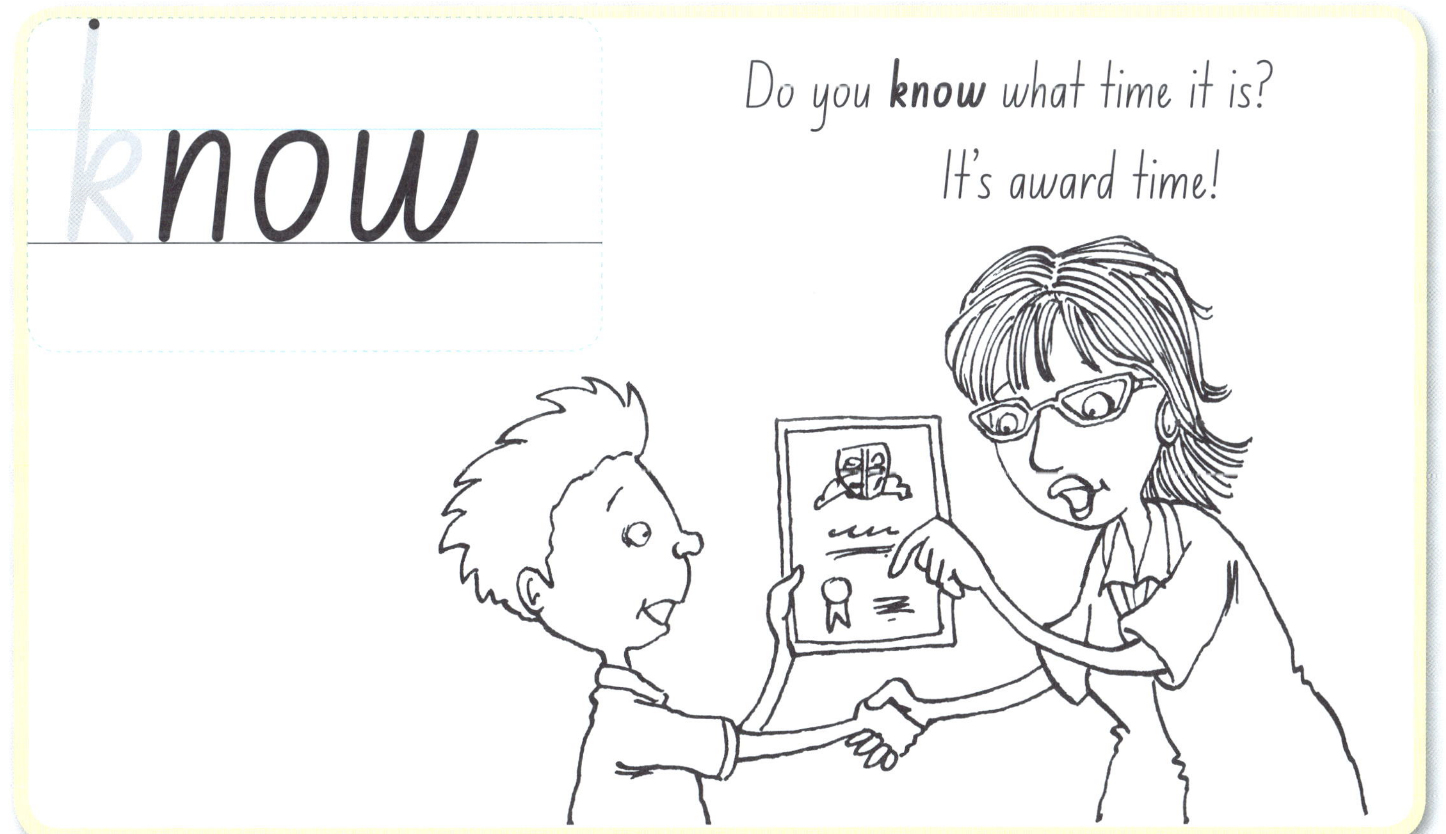

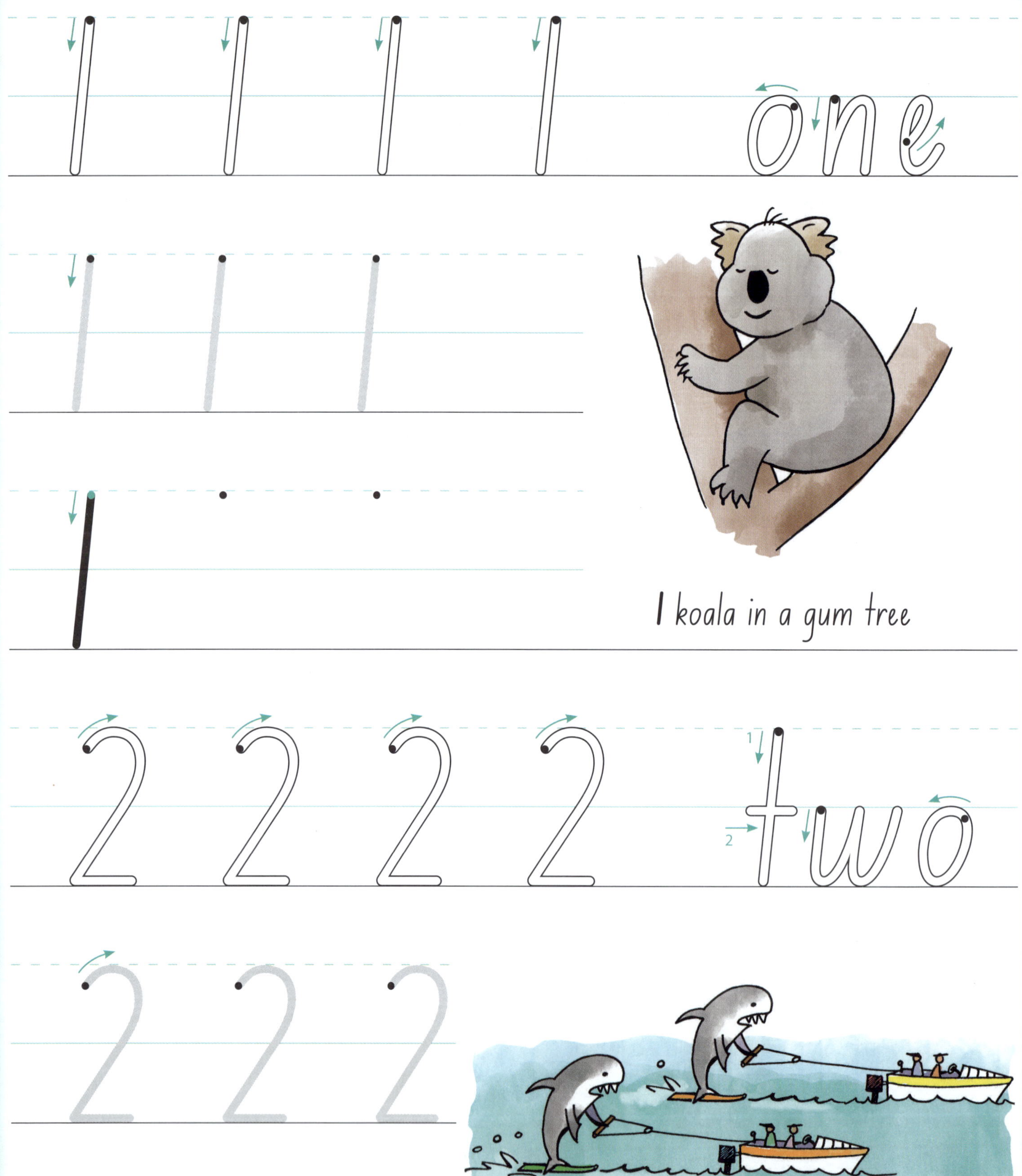

1 koala in a gum tree

2 sharks on skis

3 kangaroos

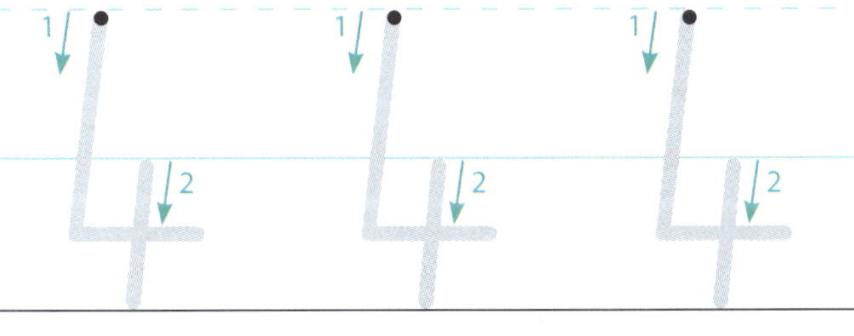

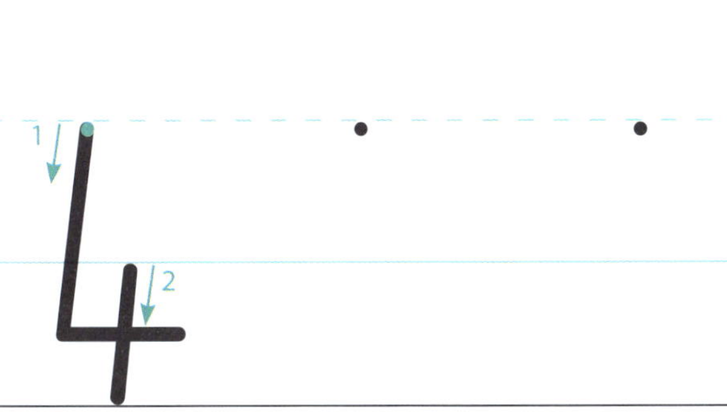

4 emus

5 lyrebirds

6 spiders spinning

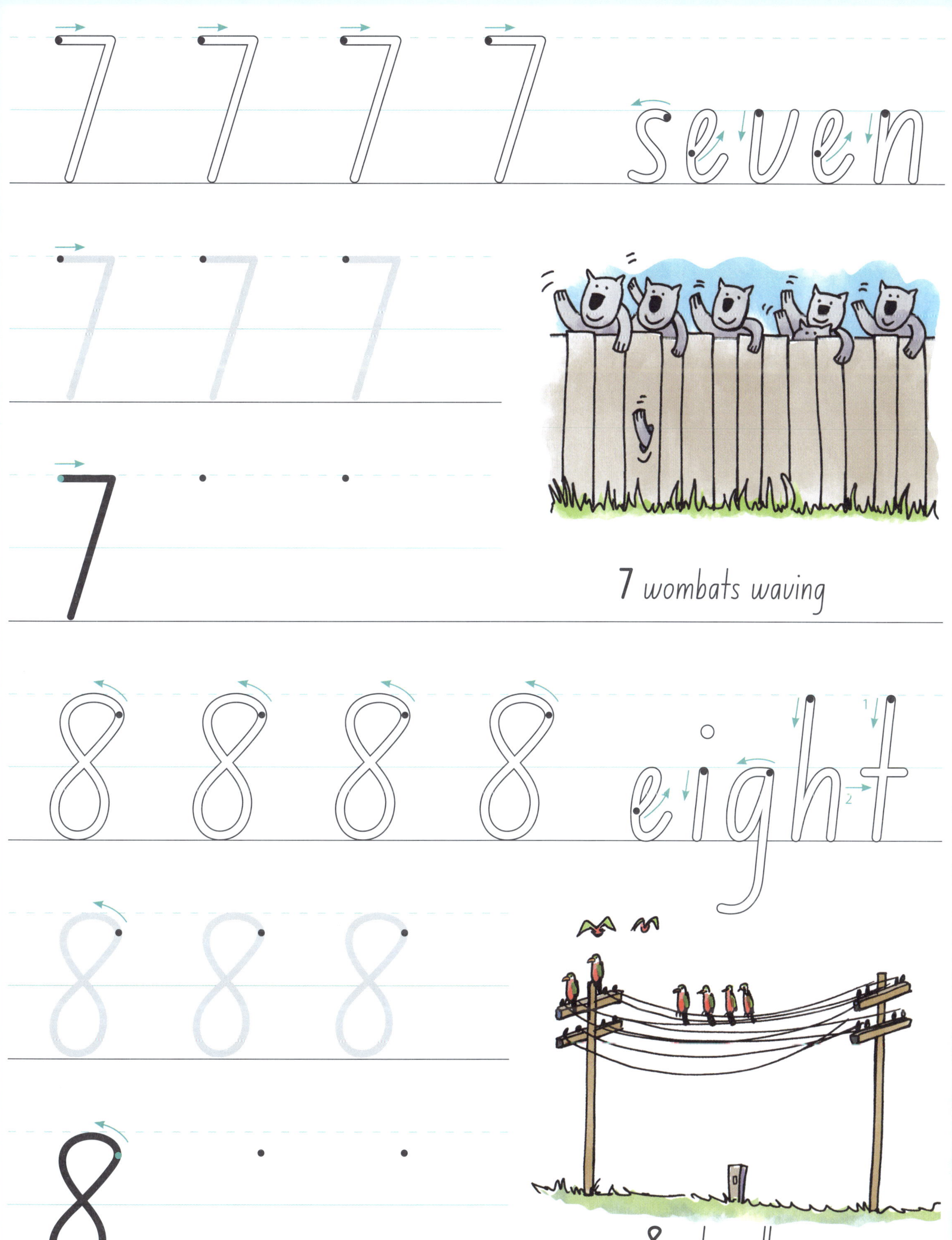

7 wombats waving

8 red rosellas

q q q q
nine
q q q
q
PLEASE WAIT TO BE SEATED
WATERHOLE CAFE
9 crocodiles
10 10 10
ten
10 10 10
10
10 dolphins diving

10

9

8

7

6

5

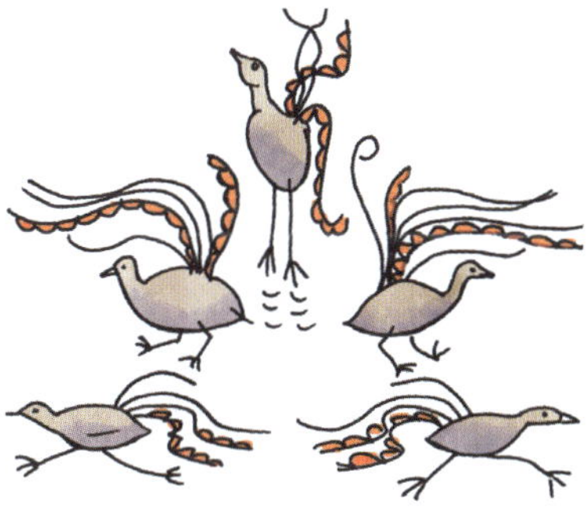

4

3

2

1 one

I koala in a tree!

a b c d e f g h i

j k l m n o p q r

s t u v w x y z

A B C D E F G H I

J K L M N O P Q R

S T U V W X Y Z